Self Storage 101 has the exclusive rights to reproduce this work, to prepare derivative works from this work, to publicly distribute this work, to publicly perform this work and to publicly display this work.

All rights reserved. No part of this book may be reproduced or transmitted in any form or by any means, electronic or mechanical, including photocopying, recording, or by any information storage and retrieval system, without permission from Self Storage 101.

Printed in the United States of America.

Contents

Forward 5
Chapter 1 10
   The Axis of Evil: Why Self Storage Managers Fail to Succeed 10
Chapter 2 15
   Characteristics of a Successful Manager 15
Chapter 3 17
   Why do you need an effective sales presentation? 17
   Competitive Market Place 19
   Rule of Thirds 21
   An Effective Phone Sales Presentation 24
Chapter 4 26
   Why do people need a storage unit? ... 26
   Why a particular site? 28
   Why do people quit storing? 29
   Additional Reasons Customers Choose a Storage Facility 31
   Convenience & Location 31
   Security 32
   Price 33
Chapter 5 36

Six Steps to a Great Sales Presentation 36
Step 1: Getting Ready 37
Step 2: First Impressions 39
Effectively using Price Stalls................ 45
Step 3: Discovering needs 49
Step 4: Building Value by Solving Problems.. 53
Cross Selling.. 60
Step 5: Overcoming Objections............ 64
Step 6: Closing the Sale: Another Satisfied Customer............................... 67
Effective Closes 68
What if You Are Not Able to Close........ 70
BONUS! 71
Using the 'Yes-or-Yes' sales skill to rent more space and sell more stuff!.......... 71
Chapter 6... 73
The Art of Collecting More Rent........... 73
Why Collections Are Important........ 73
What if it were your money?................ 78
The Collection Process Starts Early . 79
Steps to Effective Collection Calls.... 80
Effective collection calls 81
Watch what you say........................... 89

Types of Collections Calls 91
    Documentation 96
    Okay, Now They're Really Mad 97
Documentation 98
BONUS! 102
    Using Auto-Debit to Reduce Collections 102
Chapter 7 103
    Effective Tools to Getting It All Done 103
        Where do you find the time? 103
        Learning with a Time Management Exercise 105
        Time Management Tips 106
Conclusion 112

Forward

In the past thirty years, countless owners, operators, and facility managers have found their 'calling' in the business of self-storage. Self-storage is an industry that people from all walks of life can and do find satisfying work.

Self-storage is also a highly manager-centered business. There are few business models in which the success or failure of the business is so clearly and intricately intertwined with the manager's skills, personality, customer service attitude and common sense.

Unfortunately, the self-storage 'landscape' consists of a large number of multi-million dollar assets (the facilities) in the hands of people (managers) who have no business holding the keys. And unfortunately, these assets are owned by people who have invested large amounts of money hoping for a miracle but who spend more time playing golf and having lunch with their pals than providing training and other tools of success for their managers.

Many businesses are product or service driven, with their success dependent on a specific product or service. But the self-storage business is, for the most part, reliant on the manager's ability to determine customer needs and offer a viable storage solution.

Over the past several years in the self-storage industry, no one's job importance or skill set has changed more than that of the onsite manager. In the beginning of the self storage industry, the pre-21st Century manager could be, and often was, merely a 'caretaker, leaf-raker and order-taker.' It was a person whose primary responsibilities included keeping the facility clean and renting units to prospective tenants that called or came by the office. In today's competitive arena, that role has changed.

The self-storage industry has changed, both in competitiveness and customer expectations. In today's market, no longer can self-storage facilities 'make do' with a poorly trained, incompetent manager, who has neither the tools nor the inclination to succeed.

Owners or managers that insist on 'doing things the way we always have' will find themselves falling to the back of the pack. With advancements in marketing plans, the sales and collections skill set, customer relations training, and revenue management systems, today's manager must be on the cutting edge of the industry in order to survive.

While little has changed in the technical skills needed to functionally operate a self-storage facility, as it relates to using the software management system, filing the paperwork and keeping up with minor maintenance issues, much has changed in the type of manager needed to effectively compete in the 21st Century and much has changed in the critical tools they need to succeed.

Before 1990, the prototypical self-storage onsite manager was typically a semi-retired person with some management experience and the ability to take care of normal wear-and-tear maintenance of a self-storage facility. Management normally took the form of a 'team' comprised of a husband and a wife.

Since the husband usually took care of the property, while the wife took care of the office, owners and operators accepted any shortcomings from one or both and learned to 'settle'.

While it has always been important to rent space and collect money, rarely were those functions stressed as *the* primary responsibility of the management team, and rarely did owners and operators treat those functions as consistent priorities in their regular communications with their onsite managers. It is still important to keep an organized office and a spotless property but they mean very little if the spaces are not rented. Finding a balance is a goal for every manager.

There are many resources available to the self-storage manager as it relates to how to efficiently manage an office, how to keep the property in tip-top shape, and how to legally sell a unit at a lien auction. Nevertheless, the 21st Century self-storage professional manager, in order to be highly successful in increasing revenues, profits, and asset values must learn and utilize a new, more modern set of skills.

For years, self-storage onsite managers could, and often did, rent storage space despite themselves. Fortunately, the supply and demand realities often allowed for 'dumb luck' space rentals. The self-storage business was good, revenues were adequate, and distribution checks were sent in on time. Very little attention was paid to maximizing the facilities potential.

Now, in order to effectively compete, a 21st Century self-storage professional must actively 'sell' their storage solutions to an ever discriminating customer base, use proven collection techniques to maximize the potential income percentages, and learn to use effective time management skills to get it all done. This workbook is designed to provide today's self-storage professional the tools he or she needs to succeed at the highest levels of success.

Chapter 1

The Axis of Evil: Why Self Storage Managers Fail to Succeed

In the last two decades of working in self-storage facilities and interacting with countless self-storage managers, I have noted very few who aren't conscientious, hard-working individuals. Most are caring people who celebrate the successes of increasing occupancies and revenues, and agonize over empty storage units, decreased truck rentals and poor packing supply sales.

While it is likely that the manager is not entirely at fault should a particular facility fail to experience expected rentals, there are clearly critical tools that far too many managers either have not been provided or consistently fail to use. This lack of 'tool utilization' is the primary cause of lackluster results or imminent failure of a self-storage facility.

There are three primary 'tools' a self-storage manager must have to succeed in the increasingly competitive market. The inability for managers to use these tools effectively and successfully can have grave consequences on their self-storage facility:

Tool #1 - Effective Sales Skills

The days are gone when a self-storage manager was expected to successfully rent self-storage space with little or no training. Today's self-storage professional must be provided the following high level training:

- Conducting effective phone and in-store sales presentations.
- Selling each potential tenant on the value of renting space at their facility.
- How to greet customers, offer features and benefits, and use price stalls.
- Handling customer objections
- Using an effective lead management system

- Conducting successful prospect follow-ups- especially those that haven't made a storage decision.

Tool #2 - Effective Collections Techniques

While some managers may be 'born' sales persons, I've never met anyone who was a born 'collector'. Far too many self-storage managers do not know how to successfully manage their collections process and clearly do not understand their critical role in maximizing collections.

An effective collection effort comes from using a proven system that ensures consistency and fairness and one that allows managers to clearly understand their responsibilities. While no one likes to work on collections, it is something every successful manager must do. Even though the space may be rented, the facility doe not benefit unless money is actually collected.

I have found that if a professional self-storage manager 'treats' the money like his or her own, the collection effort is more consistent, there is a greater commitment, and a pronounced sense of urgency. If given the proper tools and training, a professional manager is more likely to succeed.

Tool# 3 -Effective Time Management Processes

Some managers have developed a long list of excuses to explain why they have not completed certain tasks. The tasks may include failing to address a customer service issue, failure to maintain the proper paperwork, or maintaining the appearance of the facility. Since so much time is wasted during the day, many managers turn in hours of overtime to complete certain requirements.

If a manager is organized, prepared, and focused, there is no excuse for a failure to maintain all aspects of the facility within the normal business hours.

Research clearly indicates that when professional onsite managers were provided the tools and training needed, they were more productive, less stressed, and more likely to provide outstanding customer service. A manager that can 'have a life' outside the business is also more likely to prevent burnout and maintain a positive attitude at work.

Providing a high level of intensive onsite manager training in sales, collections, and time management is, for the owner or operator, an investment in their employees and their assets.

Notes:

Chapter 2

Characteristics of a Successful Manager

The 21st Century self-storage professional is likely to have sales or customer service background and a clear understanding of the importance of renting space and collecting rent. The 21st Century self-storage professional is, in fact, a professional. Not only does he or she conduct himself in a professional manner, he understands the importance of appearance, attitude, and work-ethic.

More than ever, it is important that today's onsite manager have an outgoing personality. Customers are becoming more discerning about storage solutions; therefore those who can relate to their customers clearly have an 'edge' in the marketplace.

With such a substantial amount of capital invested in the typical self-storage facility it behooves an owner to select a manager that can successfully run his facility.

They should be able to take full ownership in the business, represent the facility at Chamber of Commerce meetings, and know how to market to professional offices, small retail shops, and apartment complexes.

Qualities of a Successful manager
- A pleasing and well-groomed appearance
- The manager should have a professional demeanor
- An outgoing personality, with a genuine love for other people
- He/she must be organized and detail oriented
- The manager should be self-motivated and driven
- A sense of pride and ownership in the business
- A servant's heart, always putting the customer first

Ultimately, the 21st Century manager must be able to use effective techniques to turn more prospects into tenants. He must also follow an efficient collection system, and implement a time management process to work smarter, not harder.

Chapter 3

Why do you need an effective sales presentation?

The 21st Century self-storage professional must first realize that he or she must treat the rental of storage space as the top priority each and every day. Without renting storage spaces, other job functions become far less important. After all, a very clean but empty storage facility is of little value to anyone.

What if you could use a few proven sales skills to rent just one more unit per week next year with no additional expense? Would it make a difference? If so, how much?

Let's Look at the Math

- If the average unit rents for $120 per month and the average length of stay is 10 months then the average value of each rental is $1200.
- By renting one extra unit each week, that's an extra 52 units each year.
- By multiplying $1200 X 52, we see that it adds up to an additional $62,400 in rental income.
- A $62,400 increase in rental income would equal an approximate increase in facility value of $780,000

As you can see, one extra rental per week really does matter! When you understand the value of each rental, and just as importantly, the cost of not renting a space, you will learn to have a 'sense of urgency'.

That awareness helps to understand the importance of 'dropping everything' when the opportunity to make a sale arises. Managers who understand this principle and use it have a competitive advantage in the market.

Competitive Market Place

Not only do effective sales presentations yield greater income, they are also vital to the success of a self-storage facility. No longer does 'build it and they will come' suffice as a marketing strategy. This is especially true since the market place has become so competitive. Today's professional self storage manager must have a better understanding of what customers want and they must use up-to-date marketing skills to be successful.

Interesting Facts

- The average self storage customer contacts three to five facilities before making a decision. The customers are more sophisticated and better informed about their options.

- They are more interested in value, which is not the same as the cheapest.
- Over eighty-five percent of all self storage customers will make a call before visiting a site, especially since no one has the time to drive around and shop for storage.
- People are aware they have many storage facility choices.
- Over ninety percent of all self storage customers will rent from someone. Why not you? Keep in mind that customers are not shopping for the fun of it. Don't miss your opportunity to rent a unit. Make every sales presentation count.
- Self-storage is a need-driven market, not a casual purchase. Assume that every potential customer will rent a space.
- Most customers think all self-storage is the same. Make sure your sales presentation explains why your facility is different- better.

> "IT IS CRITICALLY IMPORTANT TO NOTE: MOST PEOPLE THAT SHOP FOR STORAGE END UP RENTING STORAGE. RENT THEM A UNIT OR ONE OF YOUR COMPETITORS WILL!"

Rule of Thirds

A great deal of consumer research and habits has been gleaned from the countless number of phone calls that third-party call centers have taken over the years. Their research indicates consistent patterns in the phone calls of prospective self-storage customers:

- One-third of prospective tenants contact a storage facility with a specific site in mind- yours! Perhaps they have rented from you before? Maybe they were referred by a friend or family member? Fortunately, the quality, or lack thereof, of your sales presentation will likely have little bearing on their decision.

- One-third will not rent from you for any reason. It could be you don't have the space or size they need? Perhaps your facility is just too far from their home? Maybe your facility doesn't have a particular amenity needed to meet their needs. Unfortunately, no matter how effective your sales presentation may be, it will likely not have an impact on their decision.

- One-third might rent from you if you can sell the customer on the value of storing at your facility. Since this person is seeking a storage solution, your sales ability will determine whether or not this person rents from your facility. Never take this customer for granted, making sure you sell them on your value. If you don't someone else will.

When the phone rings or a potential customer walks into your facility, how do you know into which of these categories a particular customer falls? You can't.

This is why it is important that you assume every customer is in the 'third' that might just rent from you if you can 'sell' them on the value of your facility.

What is your success rate? Of the prospects that call or come by your facility, how many are you renting to? Do you track customer contacts and calculate your closing percentage? If not, why not? Every successful manger should have a goal of renting to at least 65% of their prospects. The value of each rental demands that each lead is treated 'like gold'. Every potential customer should experience your best sales presentation.

Why is renting storage space a manager's top priority? With such a large investment, it's simply too expensive to have empty spaces. Consider the costs of not renting storage space:

- The company spent money trying to get the phone to ring. If people call and we don't rent them space, we will not be successful.
- Obviously, it creates a loss in rental income

- If we don't rent space, we lose our opportunity for merchandise sales and truck rentals
- Without customers, we lose customer referrals
- Revenue is lost to pay for utilities, security, and salaries

An Effective Phone Sales Presentation

All self-storage facilities invest in various forms and channels in order to market their business. Although those efforts take on diverse forms, they all have one thing in common. Take a look at the following to see if you can find that one common denominator:

- Yellow pages
- Website
- Flyers
- Signage
- Business cards
- Rental trucks
- Craigs List and other classified ads

If you guessed a telephone number, you are correct. If we want our clients to call, it only makes sense that we make sure our number gets into their hands. Unless they come to your facility, the only way to make a sell is to get them to call. When clients do call, make sure you have a designated plan and a specific outcome. Never 'wing it'.

Why is a manager's phone presentation so important? Let's take a look at the advantages of an effective presentation:

- It helps to convert a higher percentage of your prospects.
- It doesn't require additional resources to rent more space.
- You can expect to see immediate results
- Provides a greater chance of getting the client to the site, thus increasing your chance to sell value, rent space, rent trucks, and sell merchandise. Getting them to the site requires a greater level of commitment. A self-storage space cannot be rented over the phone.

- Keep in mind that the 'sales' presentation isn't the same as a 'lease' presentation. A sales presentation gets them to the site, while the lease presentation explains the rules and regulations of your company. Never conduct the lease presentation until the client is officially a customer.

"THE GOAL OF AN EFFECTIVE SALES PRESENTATION IS TO GET THE PROSPECT INTO YOUR SITE."

Chapter 4

Why do people need a storage unit?

Self-storage is a 'need-driven' business and understanding why people choose to store helps the self-storage professional work to meet those needs. Some of those reasons include:

- When people move to a new home, or town, they often need temporary storage.
- Families that merge often need extra storage space.
- Families often need storage to house holiday decorations, or other items that won't fit into their garages or closets.
- When couples go through a divorce, they often need rental space while they are re-locating or building.
- Businesses often need storage to house files, surplus furniture, or other supply items.
- When kids leave and come back home, storage space is often needed to store everything.
- When relatives die, storage is sometimes needed to preserve clothes, furniture, and other keepsake items.

Why a particular site?

With a large number of self-storage facilities in most markets, consumers are forced to make a decision on where to store their items. What factors influence a client's choice? What features or benefits are customers looking for when renting?

- There are four primary reasons a prospective tenant chooses a self-storage site:
    o Manager's professionalism
    o Convenience and/or location
    o Perceived Security
    o Price and/or value

Although each reason plays an important role, the number one factor is the manager's level of professionalism. A recent survey indicated customers are drawn to storage facilities because of the confidence generated by their initial contact with the site manager. Consumers are looking for managers who convey they genuinely care about their situation and their stored items.

Why do people quit storing?

While most customers stop renting because they no longer require the services of a particular self-storage facility, it is important to realize there may be other reasons that affect their decision, such as:

- Price. Is your facility still competitive with other facilities in your area?
- Death
- Moved to a new location
- Relationship with the manager

While some of these reasons are out of our control, we should be concerned about pricing and manager relationship. Are our prices still comparable to others? What happened to damage the relationship with management? What can we learn from this? What would we do differently next time?

Of all the reasons people no longer use a storage facility's services, the attitude of the manager was the number one reason for many customers.

In a recent study of retail businesses, sixty-eight percent of respondents stated that manager indifference was the primary reason they no longer did business with a particular business.

It is imperative that the manager understands and accepts his/her role and responsibility. The manager is the key to every facility's success.

Negative Effects of Manager Indifference

- Word of mouth can be good or bad, depending on the attitude of the manager. Unfortunately, negative feedback often travels faster and farther than positive feedback. When people have a bad experience, they feel the need to tell others. Some wish to 'save' others from the same treatment, while others simple want to vent about their problem.
- Loss of a return customer
- Taints all self-storage managers as being uncaring and indifferent

Additional Reasons Customers Choose a Storage Facility

Convenience & Location

In self-storage surveys, customers often say they chose a particular site simply because they saw it when they drove by the business on the way to and from their home. People want to store their goods in a location that is convenient to them and their busy lifestyle. They don't want their stored items locked away in a remote location. Because so many potential customers will decide to rent from your site because they 'saw it' it is important for you to make sure:

- The facility is well-maintained
- The business has an inviting curb appeal
- Clear signage with a phone number

In many ways, the self-storage industry is similar to the apartment industry. Most tenants make up their mind about renting when they first pull up- appearance matters.

Curb Appeal Checklist:

- Is the facility nicely landscaped? Are the shrubs and bushes well manicured?
- Are the bollards in need of painting?
- Are the unit doors dirty or damaged?
- Is the front door clean and/or freshly painted?
- Is the signage appealing?

Security

Since prospective tenants want to feel that their goods will be safe, it is important that the facility manager build trust with each client. This trust begins by getting to know each customer, carefully listening to their needs, and explaining the factors and benefits of the facility. The more trust you establish with your customers the more you increase their perceived sense of security about your site.

Things to Remember

- Point out 'secure' features of your site
    - perimeter fencing
    - 24 hour lighting
    - Key pad access
    - Onsite manager
    - Video surveillance
    - Alarmed units
    - Each client gets his/her own lock and key

Even though it is important to discuss security features which help to separate your facility from your competitors, always refrain from guaranteeing security. If people really want to break into a facility, there is a good chance they will be successful. While most security features discourage would-be robbers, they do not prevent them.

Price

Oftentimes, onsite managers are only concerned about pricing, believing that is what customers want and are most concerned about.

Price is certainly a factor in renting storage space, but what most customers are looking for is value. Customers work hard for their money and realize the cheapest is not always the best, especially when their storage items are expensive or sentimental.

How do managers sell 'value' to potential customers? Successful managers focus their sales presentations on facility features and benefits, not just a cheap price. Without offering facility features and benefits, you are doing potential customers a disservice.

Many customers are actually willing to pay a little extra if the benefits outweigh the price. Facilities that are low-balled by surrounding storage businesses must make sure their sales presentation contains those unique features that compensate for the cheaper prices.

What Customers Want

A recent survey by a southeastern self-storage management company asked the question: 'Why did you decide to store at this particular site?'

- Sixty-two percent chose the site because of the convenience of the site to their home or business
- Twenty-two percent said they rented because of a friend or family member referral
- Eight percent stated they picked the site out of the phone book
- Thirteen percent said they chose a particular site because it was clean
- Twelve percent said they needed a particular amenity
- Only nine percent rented from a particular site due to price

Chapter 5

Six Steps to a Great Sales Presentation

The self-storage professional is charged with learning and utilizing proven sales skills in order to increase their ability to rent more storage space. While some effort should be placed in increasing the number of phone calls, walk-ins, and web leads, most self-storage professionals would greatly increase their occupancy and revenue levels by learning to convert more of their current leads into tenants.

There are six important steps in the professional sales presentation process:

> Step 1: The preparation- getting prepared for the presentation
> Step 2: Greeting the customer- first impressions are so important
> Step 3: The inquiry- discovering the needs of the client
> Step 4: Building value- assisting the client in solving problems

Step 5: Overcoming objections- selling features, benefits, and value
Step 6: Closing the sale- another satisfied tenant

Step 1: Getting Ready

Never allow tenants to serve as your test subjects. It is critical that the self-storage professional is prepared before the phone rings or the prospective tenant walks into the office. It is possible that you may only have one chance to make a lasting impression on the customer. Successful managers make every opportunity count.

- Training
    - Learn everything there is to know about your facility: how many units, square footage of each unit, security benefits, rental agreement, services, merchandise, pricing, and truck rental policies and procedures. (Almost thirty percent of all self-storage customers rent a truck.)

- Know as much about your competition as you do your own facility. Why is your facility better? Are they running special promotions? Do they have any available space for rent? What are their amenities?
- Learn from other successful storage facilities. What are they doing and why is it working? Is it curb appeal, pricing, or other unique amenities?
- Practice your presentation before your calls and reflect after each one. Did you rent or did the customer walk? What went well? What didn't? What might you do to improve? Did the client ask a question I couldn't answer? If so, more research is needed before your next phone presentation.

Baseball players, the highest paid athletes in the world, attend spring training every year. Why?

Because they have to get caught up on the latest techniques, knock the rust off, and get ready for the first game of the new season. Professional athletes don't wait to practice until 'the game is on the line,' and neither should a professional self-storage manager.

Since ninety-percent of the people shopping for storage are going to rent from someone, we must gain their business or one of our competitors will. How do we make sure our customers don't walk?

Step 2: First Impressions

The way a prospective tenant is initially greeted either on the phone or in the store will have a direct bearing on whether he rents from you or your competitors. What you say and how you say it means everything. Most customers can quickly tell if you are genuine and appreciative of their business. Are you sincere about wanting their business? Do you sound as if they are wasting your time?

How to Present An Effective Phone Greeting

- Be prompt, clear, and friendly
    o Customers can tell whether or not you like your workplace based on how you answer the phone. If you don't like your job, they will know.
- Don't be in a hurry. Take your time with each customer, making sure you speak slowly and answer all questions.
- Don't eat a meal, text friends, or play a game of Solitaire on the computer. Focus on what the customer is saying and think about how you plan to respond.
- Thank the customer for calling you and ask, 'How may I help you?'
    o Remember, they have many other choices for their storage needs.
- Smile before answering the phone. Your smile and out-going personality will show up in your voice.

- People prefer to interact with someone who is genuinely friendly and happy. Make sure your client can identify with you.
- Politely ask the caller if he/she has rented with you before. Collecting this information will allow you to personalize the presentation and make the most effective use of the caller's time. If they have rented before, you can skip a large portion of the sales presentation.

Collect Vital Caller Information

It is interesting that so many self-storage managers are reluctant to ask a potential customers' name and phone number. Try asking, 'By the way, who am I speaking to?' or 'In case we get disconnected, how can I reach you?' I have never had anyone respond 'I'm not telling you who I am!'

Using the Prospect's Name

- Doing so personalizes the call
    - Lets the customer know that you care about who they are
- People love to hear their name used
    - Try to use their name 2-3 times during the conversation
- Shows respect for the most important person in our business- the customer
- Never use caller ID to re-call a customer. You may be calling them at a number they would prefer not to be called, or at a number they are not allowed to take calls
    - They may have been calling from work but wish to be called at home
    - An estranged spouse might be making inquiries about needing storage space and a return call to their caller ID might prove problematic

Using An Effective In-Store Greeting

While similar in scope, there are differences in the mechanics between a phone greeting and an in-store greeting.

- Start with a 'Good Morning or Good Afternoon!'
    - People like to do business with a happy person
    - Lets person know you are glad they are at your facility and not an interruption of your day
- Offer your name and ask for theirs.
    - Use their name throughout the presentation.
    - Lets customers know you are listening to them and trying to get to know them better.
- Thank the prospect for choosing to stop by your facility
    - Understand that the prospective customer has many choices

- - o Let them know you genuinely appreciate them giving you the opportunity to tell them about your facility.
- Stand up to greet a customer
  - o Shake hands and look them in the eyes
  - o Meet them at the door if possible
- Be friendly and engaging. Try to evoke a smile.
  - o 'You must really need some boxes today to come out in this rain!'
  - o 'You must really need a truck today to want to move on such a beautiful day!'
- Let the customer know you want to help solve their problem
  - o Remember that the customer has a specific storage need and is reaching out to you to meet that need
- Be empathetic with their concerns
  - o Listen, understand, and repeat what they told you. Don't interrupt them.

- Attempt to establish rapport with the tenant
    - Prospective customers want to feel comfortable with the person who will be responsible for protecting their worldly goods and valuable items.
- Start the conversation with an open-ended question
    - 'So, when will you need storage?'
    - "Have you decided how to move your goods into storage?'
    - 'Are all of your goods packed, or do you still have some to go?'

Effectively using Price Stalls

Oftentimes the first question a potential customer will ask is 'how much'? Far too often, managers answer with a price. As I have stated earlier, managers are doing their customers a disservice by quoting a price without offering your business' features and benefits.

Instead of quoting a price, especially when you know your price is a little high, consider saying, 'I'll be glad to give you a price. Before I do, please allow me to share some of our features and benefits, which will allow you to compare apples to apples' or 'Before I give you our price, please allow me the opportunity to tell you what our price includes.'

Would you consider buying a gift-wrapped box without first knowing what was in the box? Without knowing what's in the box, most of us would not be willing to pay very much. We are asking our customers to do the same thing when we only tell them the price. They know how much it costs, but have no idea about what they get for the money.

What's in the box? What makes you unique and/or different?

- Add up the benefits
  - Make sure your prospective customer knows the benefits of 'buying your box'.

The more benefits you add to the 'box' the more you relieve the pressure to have the lowest rates.
- Subtract the competitive disadvantages
  - It is important that you know about your competitors and some of their disadvantages without disparaging those competitors; you are trying to meet a storage need and there may be reasons your competitors cannot meet those needs
- Multiply the intangibles
  - What is it about you and your storage facility that would make the difference between you and your competitors?
  - "One of the features we offer is quality service and people who care. We want to do so well that you come back to us, should the need arise and be so good at what we do that you call a friend."

- Divide the difference
    - What if you are $10 higher per month than your closest competitor? That equals 30 cents a day. Do you believe you and your facility are worth an extra 30 cents a day?
    - Do you have unique amenities to help in justifying the extra money, such as security, more reasonable merchandise (boxes, bubble wrap, tape), or a more convenient and accessible location?

Additional Effective Price Stalls:

- 'Let me get my price list. While I'm doing that, let me ask you a few questions.'
    - ❑ This allows you to launch right into your sale presentation
- 'Since availability affects pricing, let me ask you how soon you will need the unit.'

- ❑ Again, this allows you to launch into your sales presentation without sounding 'pushy'
- 'So that I can save you the most money, let me ask you a few questions.'
  - ❑ Who doesn't want to save money?

Step 3: Discovering needs

It is important that the self-storage professional properly assesses the customer's needs before recommending a solution.

- Never start an inquiry by asking 'what size do you need?' or 'Do you need any boxes?' or 'Do you need a truck?'
  - o 'Yes or No' questions result in 'Yes or No' answers- usually 'No'
  - o Start a conversation with the customer

- By asking 'what size do you need?' you are abdicating your role as the self-storage professional and asking the customers to solve his or her own storage needs. Keep in mind that if you ask this question and they answer with a specific size, it is likely that another inexperienced or uncaring self-storage manager told them the size they needed. Keep in mind, there may be no correlation between the size they believe they need and the size they do need. Have you ever answered someone's 'how much is your 10x10?' with a price and then had them show up in a 26 foot Uhaul truck; those items are not going to fit in a 10x10 and you now have an upset customer.
- Personalize the experience by asking customer-specific questions; be curious!
    - 'So, if your son is moving home, how long will you need the storage unit?'
    - "Do you sell a lot of stuff on eBay, or is this a one-time thing?'

- 'I know those apartments; are you moving upstairs or downstairs?'
- Ask open ended questions; WHAT, WHEN and WHY?
    - Allow the prospect to tell their story
- Ask probing questions to get more specific
    - The only way to truly assess the customer's needs is to ask questions.
        - Establish your expertise
- Listen to how the customer responds to your questions. Pay attention!
- If you are not paying attention to the answers, you send the message that you are not interested in the customer's needs. You will also lose trust quickly.
- If a customer needs to buy boxes or rent a truck you need to ask what they plan to do with them. For example, books should not be packed in large boxes and a 16 foot rental truck is not large enough for all the contents of a 4 bedroom house.

- If they bring up security concerns, they are probably not interested in your free Starbucks coffee. Listen to their concerns and address those specific concerns.
- The more questions you ask, the more you confirm that you are the expert and the customer made the right decision contacting you.
- Focus on the features the customer is looking for and use 'soft closes'
    - Your presentation does not have to cover every amenity and service you offer; listen for the customer's 'hot buttons'.
    - Soft closes are helping the customer to agree with you:
        - 'So you WILL need climate control?'
        - 'So you WILL need the rental truck on Thursday?'
        - 'So one bundle of medium boxes should be adequate?'

- o By getting the customer to agree, they affirm that they will rent or buy.
- Listen for buying signals
  - o Whenever the prospect starts asking questions about money, availability, or timing, they are sending 'buying signals'.
  - o 'Do you take VISA'?
  - o 'Do you have one of those available?'

Step 4: Building Value by Solving Problems

After using an inviting greeting and listening to the customer to determine their storage needs, you are now in a position to 'build value' in storing with your facility. By offering pertinent features and benefits that clearly define the advantages you have in your competitive marketplace, you can 'tip the scales' from price to value.

"OFFERING MORE FEATURES AND BENEFITS REDUCES THE PRESSURE TO HAVE THE LOWEST PRICES!"

Features and Benefits

- Your sales presentation has to include a discussion about features *and* benefits.
  - FEATURES
  - A list of the amenities and services your facility provides
    - Onsite manager
    - Perimeter fencing
    - Wide driveways
    - Security cameras
    - Climate control
    - 24 hour access
    - Restricted key pad access
  - Yourself- it is important to send the message that you are more caring, more personable than your competitors
  - Point out brochure bullet points
  - Location- Why is your location better than your competitors?

- BENEFITS
- Clearly explains what each feature does to enhance the storage experience or why the benefit is important.
- The manager should discuss the 'why' a prospective tenant would care about or want a particular feature and the 'what's in it for me' aspect.
- The manager should carefully transition from a feature to a benefit by using 'so that':
  - Our units are climate controlled 'so that' your goods are protected from heat and humidity.
  - We have restricted keypad access 'so that' you can rest-assured that only our tenants are able to access to the property.
  - Remember, a large percentage of prospective customers have never used self-storage before.

- Don't take for granted the customer will understand the various features and how they can meet their particular storage needs

Showing Storage Units

Showing a storage unit to the prospective tenant is a critical step in the sales process. Let's look at some important things to remember:

- Always show your 'least desirable' units first. When you start at the least desirable units you are presenting them as perfectly 'usable' spaces instead of relegating them to the 'last resort' category if a customer cannot afford the more expensive desirable spaces.
    - Upstairs
    - Non-Air conditioned
    - Hallways
    - Be prepared to 'sell' the benefits of using one of the less desirable spaces:

- - 'Some of our tenants have chosen to use the storage space on the upper floors because they believe them to be more safe'
  - 'If your goods can be stored in your garage they can be stored in one of our non-climatized storage spaces, which are less expensive'
- Always offer the customer choices, always showing at least three units.
  - Be prepared. Know what spaces are vacant and have the keys with you.
- Discuss the unique features of the property:
  - Clearly explain the keypad system to the potential customer. Always refrain from using a remote control to open the gate because if you fail to stop and use the keypad instead you miss an opportunity to 'show-and-tell' one of the important security measures at your facility.

- o Demonstrate how clean and well-kept the facility is consistently kept. Explain what great lengths you go to in order to maintain the facility and how the tenants actually help keep the site clean.
- Never mix your 'sales' presentation with your 'lease' presentation.
  - o Telling a prospective customer what will happen to their goods if their rent isn't paid is part of the lease presentation, not the sales presentation
- The property tour is also a great time to sell packing supplies. Help the customer visualize how more efficiently their unit can be packed by using certain sized boxes and mattress bags.
  - o Never ask 'Do you need any boxes?'
  - o Ask "have you started packing your items yet?'

- Allows customer to 'tell their story' and it gives the manager a chance to offer the customer more cost effective and efficient alternatives.
- If a customer says they are just going to 'get some boxes from behind the liquor store' you can point out the potential for insect infestation in those boxes, the fact those boxes might not be designed to properly pack their goods and that you never know what might have been spilled in or already put in those boxes.
- The merchandise sales presentation should continue in the office when customers can see the merchandise
- What about your rental truck?
- Never ask 'Do you need a truck?' Ask instead 'Have you decided how to get your good into storage?'
- If a customer says they are borrowing a neighbor's pick-up truck you can point out that that will mean more trips back and forth, the potential for bad weather and the potential danger of their goods being damaged.

- If you wait until the prospect shows up to rent their storage space, it's too late to rent them a truck

Cross Selling

Trucks, boxes and self-storage units fit together like the pieces of a puzzle. Not offering the items is a disservice to the customers. You are also taking a risk that the customer might buy the supplies from a competitor.

Most ancillary sales opportunities take place within the self-storage sales process and you need to incorporate these into your property tour. As you start to close the storage rental, it's now time to reinforce the 'cross sell' the other products or services you offer.

Once you have ended the property tour do not stop selling your products and services.
- Offer locks, insurance, truck rentals and merchandise

- Move-in price should ALWAYS include lock & insurance. ASSUME the sale and let the customer tell you 'no', that they don't need something. If you first give them a move-in price that only includes the rent and then try to add additional costs on top of that it becomes a harder sell.
- It is Important that you have highly Effective Retail Displays
    - Items must be Clean
    - Items must be clearly priced
    - Your display need to looks full
- Lots of Inventory stacked chest high throughout the office
    - Box bundles
    - newsprint
- Make sure you point out your competitive prices
    - You offer the convenience of a one-stop-shop
    - Selling the customer all of the items they need to complete their packing will save trips
- Point our your Buy Back Program
    - Offer to buy back unused boxes

- Insure the customer knows he can save money by purchasing bundles of boxes; they can return the ones they don't use but customers rarely return unused boxes.
- Sell bundles
  - Always offer to upsize from a few boxes to a bundle of boxes. Never sell a box without offering tape or other packing materials. Find out what the customer plans to pack.
  - Know how the various box sizes and other materials can best be used:
    - Small boxes- easy to carry and holds heavy items such as books and dishes
    - Medium boxes- clothes, small appliances, and toys
    - Large boxes- large, bulky items, lamps, and pillows
- Use Professional signage
  - No hand-made signs
  - Signs that clearly indicate types and prices of items

Locks:

During the lease presentation, explain that tenants must provide their own lock. Let them know that you have locks available for purchase in the office. Make sure to take one or two different types with you on the property tour.

- Take scissors with you on the property tour so that you can cut open the lock packaging
- 'Assume' the rental by offering to place a new lock on the tenant's space
- Don't have to make another trip back to unit
- Doing this improves time management and reduces customer service issues that arise from leaving rented units unlocked or forgetting to remove the company's lock at a later time

We highly recommend that salespersons stand near or in front of the merchandise as they are making the sales presentation.

This will give the prospective customer the impression that packing materials and other ancillary products are integrated with the space rental.

Step 5: Overcoming Objections

Despite the self-storage professional's most effective sales presentation, there are times when a prospective customer does not commit to renting a space with their first contact. It is important to realize that a 'no' or 'not right now' is not a reason to give up.

Understanding Objections:
- Objections are natural in any sales presentation and should be expected.
    - From birth, we all learn to say 'no'. It shouldn't come as a surprise when a customer says, 'no' or 'I'll have to think about it'.

- Objections come from buying customers
    - Remember that approximately ninety-percent of prospects looking for a storage solution will end up renting storage space from someone. If you don't rent them space, someone else will. Make sure you work to overcome whatever objections they have.
- Objections often mean you have not clearly understood the customer's needs.
    - When a customer is on the phone or in your office, make sure you drop everything you are doing and focus on listening and finding a solution. If you fail to meet their needs, they will take their business to a competitor.
- Objections may be signs that the customer wants to rent, but doesn't feel comfortable. Be in tune to body language and expressions to locate areas of concern.

Be quick to discuss those areas, thus easing customer stress, concern, or anxiety. Perhaps they are concerned about security?
- Be sure to focus on benefits.

When you receive objections, make sure you keep a list. By knowing what concerned past customers, you can better prepare yourself and your sales presentation for future customers.

- Price is the most common reason for an objection and one of easiest to overcome
    - Never give your price until you have established value with features and benefits
        - Use price stalls
    - Benefits increase value and decrease importance of price
    - If there is a rate difference, break it down for the customer
        - If your facility's 10x10 is $10 higher than your closest competitor, that's 30 cents a day.

Aren't you and your facility worth 30 cents a day? Again, emphasize your value benefits, and location

Step 6: Closing the Sale: Another Satisfied Customer

YOU HAVE TO ASK FOR THE SALE!

If you use an effective sales presentation, but fail to rent the space, all of your efforts were for naught. Failure to close the deal is the #1 reason people fail at sales. It is important to learn and be comfortable with two or three different closing strategies and be prepared to use them in different situations.

One tip on closing the deal is to watch for buying signals. When a customer starts asking questions that have to do with time, availability, or price, they are giving you they want to rent from you. Keep in mind that timing is critical. As soon as the customer displays a buying signal do not wait- ask for the rental.

Effective Closes

- The alternative choice close
    - Never limit a prospective tenant to one choice
    - Never give a prospect the chance to answer 'no'
        - 'Do you believe the 10x10 unit or the 10x15 unit will best meet your needs?'
        - 'Would you prefer the upstairs unit or do you believe the downstairs unit would be best for you?'
        - 'Should I reserve the truck for Thursday morning or would the afternoon be best?'

- The Last Chance close
    - Build a sense of urgency, but never be dishonest
        - 'I have one unit left in that price range; should I go ahead and reserve that unit for you today?'

- o 'This unit is on special today, but could be changed back to regular price at any time. Why don't I go ahead and reserve that now to lock in the special rate?'

- The Suggestive Close
  - o 'I suggest that we rent the space today so that you will be free to concentrate on moving in on your moving day.'

- Type of payment close
  - o 'Our customers love to rent their units with the convenience of our auto-payment program; would you prefer to use MasterCard or Visa?'

The closing style you choose is not important, but closing is! Know the styles and use the one that best matches the customer and the situation.

What if You Are Not Able to Close

There are going to be those occasions that despite your best efforts, you cannot close the sale:

- Offer to make a reservation for a later date
    - ❑ Especially if the customer is not yet ready to make a commitment
- Obtain contact information and offer to follow up at a later date
    - ❑ By securing the customer's name and phone number, you have secured the right to re-contact
- Offer to send a brochure
    - ❑ Any contact you can continue to make with the prospect is worthy of your time

BONUS!

Using the 'Yes-or-Yes' sales skill to rent more space and sell more stuff!

In sales training we teach to never ask 'yes-or-no' questions. Any question that can have a 'no' answer should be avoided since so often the customer's answer is 'no'.

Any sales question posed to a potential customer should also be a 'yes-or-yes' proposition so that whatever the customer's answer, they're a customer!

When renting space:
- 'Would you prefer the 10x10 or the 10x15?'
- 'Would you prefer the upstairs unit or the downstairs unit?'
- 'Would you prefer the climate space or the non-climate space?'

When selling moving and packing supplies:
- 'Do you need one bundle of boxes or two bundles?'
- 'Do you want the small role of bubble wrap or the large roll?'
- 'Would you prefer the cylinder lock or the disc lock?'

When offering tenant insurance:
- 'Most of our tenants find that $2000 of coverage is sufficient; do you think $2000 is enough or would you prefer a higher limit?'

When renting trucks:
- 'Would you need the truck in the morning or tomorrow afternoon?'

It is important to remember that over 90% of prospective tenants looking for storage end up renting storage space and a large percentage of those customers need packing supplies, truck rentals and tenant insurance.

Use professional 'yes-or-yes' sales skills and provide a much higher customer service experience for your tenants!

Chapter 6

The Art of Collecting More Rent

Establish Priorities

The self-storage professional has two primary responsibilities- rent space and collect money. Even though a successful manger does so much more, it doesn't change his/her primary responsibilities.

The two are completely different but go hand in hand when running a successful business. Although renting space is the highest priority, businesses who fail to maximize their collections will struggle to survive.

Why Collections Are Important

- The primary goal of collection calls is to get the customer to pay their rent on time every month.
- In the storage facility/tenant relationship, most of the responsibility to perform is on the facility.

Self-storage tenants are asked to do very little, except to help keep the facility clean and make their payments on time.
- Effective collections means: making your payroll, keeping the lights on, making repairs, or buying that new golf cart.
    o Self-storage is first and foremost a business and must be treated as such.
- Typically, self-storage units are not set up as nonprofit organizations.
    o Understand that someone invested a great deal of capital and credit to build the storage facility. Maximizing collections helps to lower risk factors.
    o The employment at self-storage facilities is possible because of the risk owners were willing to take to develop or buy the property.

Recent Industry Trends:

- Delinquencies are at all time high.
    - The stressful economy has forced many well-meaning customers to make hard decisions concerning their storage bills. Some markets are more problematic than others, due to variances in economic conditions.
- Collection problems are worse than ever.
    - For far too long managers, owners and operators have taken the ability to effectively manage collections for granted and that complacency has created a widening gap between what should be collected and what is collected.

- Managers don't want to make the call.
    - Understandably, no one likes to make collection calls, especially when they have not been provided with the proper training and tools to do so.

- Of the many facilities we have audited over the years, very few had a collections process that was both professional and effective.
    - For the most part, the collection efforts consisted of printing a past due list and making some calls when 'we get around to it'

Who's responsible for collections?

In order for a collection effort to be most effective, every storage-facility employee has to be willing to participate. An effective collections effort depends on consistency and good communication between those involved.

- Possible staff members
  - Manager
  - Assistant manager
  - Relief manager
  - Owner
  - Other

Getting Started

A self-storage facility staff's ability to effectively manage the collections process depends on the manager's attitude. Even if the onsite manager hates the collection process, he must understand that the calls must be made and he must do them in a manner that maximizes revenue collections.

- Manager attitude
  - It is of utmost importance that he/she understand the role of the manager
- Setting expectations
  - A self-storage professional learns to set personal goals and works to meet or exceed them

- 'Stick-to-it-tiveness'
    - A concerted and effective collection effort dictates that those working should stay engaged and continue until the money is collected.
    - The accounts receivable is significantly easier to maintain than it is to fix. Maintaining a regular and systematic collections effort is fundamentally critical to the successful operation of a self-storage facility.

What if it were your money?

It is important for every self-storage professional to treat the facility as if it were his/her own. When a manager treats the facility income as his own, his attitude changes and he develops a sense of urgency when collecting money. If you viewed the business as your own you would:

- Make more collections calls?
- Discontinue waiving late fees?
    - If tenants are late, unless there is an emergency, why waive the fees?
- Try to rent more and discount less?
    - Every dollar given up in rent is a dollar lost. Instead of discounts, why not learn more effective sales skills?
- Make sure the past due units were over-locked?
    - Would it be okay with you if tenants rented space and then moved out without paying?

The Collection Process Starts Early

The self-storage collections process starts as soon as the customer becomes a tenant- not when they are past due. A self-storage professional establishes customer expectations early in the sales process and reinforces those expectations throughout the tenant's relationship with the storage facility.

Steps to Effective Collection Calls

The key to collections is having a plan that is consistent and fair. A collection effort that is haphazard and irregular has very little chance of being successful.

- Make time to call
    - It is important to set aside time to make collections calls. Although your day is busy, designate a time to make calls- be intentional. Unscheduled events are typically never completed
- Once you are starting on the 3rd or 4th collection call attempt, have the tenant information sheet in front of you, not just the phone number listed on the past due report.
    - If you have made no contact with the tenant on the first one or two call attempts using the phone number on the past due list it is now time to start using additional information.

- The tenant information sheet has extra information that the tenant supplied upon first renting the space.
- It is not unusual for a phone number to become unusable after a period of time.
- Make it manageable. Set reasonable goals
    - You're NOT going to make fifty calls in one sitting
    - Split the undertaking into smaller efforts

Effective collection calls

- Identify yourself and your facility
    - Do not pretend to be someone you are not
- Verify to whom you are speaking
    - Do not discuss the customer's account with anyone but the customer
- Verify tenant's current address
    - Anytime you have a customer contact
- Your voice should be friendly but firm

- - You are not a collection agency
- Remind the customer that they agreed to pay their rent on time when they signed the lease
  - Reinforce expectations
- Always get a firm commitment with a date AND time for their payment
  - 'I'll pay when I can' is not a firm commitment
- Follow up on commitments
  - Create an expectation that you expect customers to do as they promise
- Always treat customers with respect and professionalism; never take a person's refusal to pay in a personal manner
  - Remember that it isn't about you
- Do not accept or create verbal abuse when dealing with a customer
  - There is nothing to be gained by getting into an argument with a customer

- Never leave an account-specific message on an answering machine
    - Answering machines are 'community property' and any number of people may be in a position to hear whatever message you might leave
    - The past due customer knows exactly why you are calling; therefore, there is no need to be specific when leaving messages

Don't Take It Personally

As Rick Warren says in the first line of 'A Purpose Driven Life', it's not about you. Don't take your customer's not paying on time as a personal affront against you. Keep it professional.

Customer Service Still Matters

- 'One of the deep secrets of life is that all that is really worth doing is what we do for others.' Lewis Carol

- Remember, past due tenants are still customers. How would you want to be treated?
    - The adage 'treat others the way you want to be treated' also applies to collections
    - How you treat people has long-term consequences

What's your system?

- Effective collections come from having a system.
    - While there is no 'perfect' system, every facility needs one
- Set a daily target for the number of calls you make.
    - You are much more likely to reach your goal if you set one. Track your progress each day

When do you call?

- Morning, noon and night.
    - Stagger the times you call the customer, refraining from calling at the same time each day. By alternating the time you call, you have a greater likelihood of reaching the customer, especially if he works.
- Alternate days.
    - For instance, try calling on Monday, Wednesday and Friday in the morning and Tuesday, Thursday, and Saturday in the afternoon. Change it up the following week.
- Get into a routine but not a rut. If you get into a rut you simply go thru the motions without making any progress.
    - 'A rut is a grave without an end'

- If you get into a rut your energy for making the calls will subside and you will start feeling obligated to do the 'busy' work of making the calls but have no interest in the 'effectiveness' of the calls.

Who Should You Call?

- A to Z
    - If you start with the A's, making it to the Z's will be difficult
- Do I call customers who are a week behind or only a few days?
    - If you don't get around to the 'not so late' customers, it won't be long before they are 'really late'
- Building A to Building Z
    - Split your property into sections- hallways, buildings, etc. Make sure all past due customers get phone calls on a regular basis and no one falls through the cracks
- Calls to make EVERY day?
    - Customers who lied about coming in the day before

- Failure to follow up immediately sets the tone that it's okay for your customers to tell whatever you want to hear

Making the calls

- It is important to let the customers know when they are late, especially the new customers. Give them a call the first day they are delinquent. The first day the customer is past due, give them a call.
- Utilize the information you have in the lease files, not just what's on the computer reports.
    - The past due report is usually limited to one or two phone numbers while the tenant information sheet has a great deal more information
    - There was a reason you filled out the information sheet in its entirely when the customer first became a tenant

- Check tenant info sheet for accuracy.
  - It you have called the phone number on the past due list several times and that number is 'disconnected' it is entirely possible that the phone number was input into the management software incorrectly
  - Previous audits indicate that the lists are typically not up-to-date
  - Ask for updated info when customers make payments
    - 'Do you still live at so-and-so"?
    - 'Is your phone number still so-and-so?'
- Always give the customer the benefit of the doubt at the start. You can increase your firmness in future calls, should the need arise.
  - Never lose your cool. Doing so will surely upset the very person with whom you need to establish a good relationship

- Always record the name of the person who makes a commitment for payment, along with the date the conversation took place, and the date/time of the promised payment.
    - If you don't' get the payment, call and tell them that you have not received payment as promised.
- Communicate with confidence and stay focused.
- When the customer answers, introduce yourself and tell them why you are calling. Be sure to remain business-like and courteous.
    - Allow the tenant a moment to look at his/her records.

Watch what you say

- Confirm you are talking to the correct customer.
- Never discuss account-specific details with anyone except for the tenant
- If you reach someone other than the tenant, simply leave a message for the tenant to call the facility
- Never threaten the customer.

- - Remember, you have the tenants goods secured in a storage unit. Failure to make payments on time has more potential negative consequences for the customer than for you.
- Don't offer solutions you can't fulfill.
  - Any promises or commitments must be within the company policies and procedures
  - The self-storage professional should 'own' the collection effort and does not try to 'blame' ownership for the call
- Only mention steps in process you can actually complete
  - There are very specific processes and time lines that have to be followed as regards to the lien process. Any attempt to force a past due customer to make payment, based on a lien process 'bluff', is both unprofessional and unlikely to lead to a desired outcome
- You are not a collection agency, nor the state attorney general.

Types of Collections Calls

Courtesy calls

The first calls made to past due customers should be considered 'courtesy calls', serving as a reminder to the customer that, either their rental payment will be due soon, or has just become past due.

- New customers should be called to remind them of their first payment and the date it's due.
- If the new customer is late, give them a firm, but friendly reminder that their payment is past due. These calls are most effective when the customer is between two and nine days past due.

Commitment calls

The self-storage professional is responsible for reinforcing the commitment the customer made to make his/her payments on time. Since the manager's job is not intended to be that of a collection agent, he should stress to customer the importance of paying on time.

- This call advises the customer of his/her responsibilities before the late fee is assessed.
    - The manager should remind the customer that late fees are not assessed, rather they are earned and that you do not waive late fees. It is the customer that makes the decision about whether or not to receive a late fee
    - Waiving late fees should be avoided, especially since this will only cause future problems. If the customer is late again, he/she will expect you to waive the fees as you did previously.
    - Waiving late fees can also be construed as inconsistent and unfair if the same privilege isn't awarded to everyone.
    - Never give the customer false hope that the ownership 'might' waive a late fee
- Express your concern over their account and let them know you would like to help them avoid additional charges.

- Get a firm date and time for payment.
    - It is important to confirm a date and time for the customer to make a payment. Document the commitment
    - The manager must follow-up immediately when payments are not made

Lien Calls

The self-storage customer deserves the consideration from the manager regarding the start of the lien process in which the customer could lose their goods at an auction.

Since one of the primary legal liabilities for a self-storage facility is the potential for an incorrectly processed lien sale it is incumbent on the self-storage professional to reduce this liability by reducing the potential for lien auctions. The lien calls are made to alert the customer of this probability and to work with the customer to find an alternative to the lien sale.

- Lien calls alert customers that you are beginning the process on their account. The process could result in them losing their goods.
    - Stress to the customer that you would prefer not to sell their goods at auction, but continued inaction on their part may give you no other choice
- Get a specific date and time for payment.
    - Make sure the customer understands that you expect them to keep their payment promise. Failure to do so will likely leave you no choice but to auction their goods.
- Never tell customers they are 'in lien'. That's 'industry-speak', which probably means the customer will not understand the term.
    - Although they may not understand the term, make sure they understand that if they fail to make their payment as agreed, their goods will be sold at auction

Final calls

Every manager reaches a point when everything fails and he must move to liquidate the tenant's goods at an auction. Before a unit is liquidated, it is important that the collection effort has been sufficiently documented. At least two phone calls should be made to the client, making sure they clearly understand that their time has essentially run out.

- Offer a 'deal' to keep from selling?
    - Since a lien auction is a great legal liability for a self-storage operator, it is important for the facility to try and settle with the tenant in a consistent and fair manner.
        - Keep in mind the money collected at auction is generally lower than the amount that could be collected from the tenant in a settlement. It's always better to settle.

- Let customer know the date and time their goods will be sold at auction.
  - It is important that the specifics of the lien auction time and place only be discussed with the tenant.

Documentation

In order to mitigate any potential liability from liquidating storage goods at an auction, it is important that the onsite manager fully document his or her collection efforts.

Keep a record of all notes and correspondence.
- Record all phone calls with the customer
- These notes should include dates and times, customer payment commitments, person manager spoke to and so forth.
- Good documentation provides a clear record that every attempt was taken to settle the account

Okay, Now They're Really Mad

There are times, despite your best efforts, when customers become frustrated and angry. While it is nearly impossible to eliminate these episodes, we can certainly minimize them.
- If at all possible- smile
- An aggravated customer will find it more difficult to be angry at someone smiling
- Pausing and taking a deep breath will help you maintain your control.
    - Don't over-react or respond with like explosiveness
- Try to understand the customer's point of view. Ask yourself if you have you ever felt the same way?
    - It is likely that most of us have forgotten to pay a bill, bounced a check, or had a credit card expire. Mistakes happen.
- Remain calm and refrain from calling names or threatening the customer.
    - Remember, you are likely not the reason the customers is agitated.

Documentation

While not particularly difficult in scope, there are specific documents that need to be completed by each customer. How the self-storage professional handles the implementation of these documents has a direct impact on the management of the accounts receivable.

The Tenant Information Sheet

- Be certain to collect all of the information on the customer
- The customer should fill out as much as possible, with the manager asking for and filling in any missing information. There is a reason the information is requested, and there should be an expectation that all the information be collected.
- Don't ask for an alternate contact- rather, ask for an emergency contact name and number
- When asking for an alternate contact, customers perceive it as code for 'someone we can call if you don't pay your bill'.

People are much more understanding when you ask for someone to contact in case of an emergency.
- Employer contact
    - If the person supplies a work number, you can assume it is okay to call them at work. They will usually specify when if they do not wish to be called at work.
- Ask the customer if they have any friends or family members that might be interested in storage? Let them know if you pay for referrals.
    - You are much more likely to get names and numbers of friends and families members if they know it means money in their pockets
- Be sure to get cell phone numbers and e-mail addresses.
    - Many people now use their cell phones as their primary contact.
    They may be more likely to respond to texts messages or emails than phone messages.

- It is imperative that you get a copy of their ID!
  - It is important to verify who you are renting to
- Be sure to collect all information before the customer leaves your office
  - Once a customer becomes delinquent in their payment, getting pertinent information is next to impossible

The Lease Agreement

- Be up front with each customer. Emphasize that the rent payment is due on or before their due date. The payment should be considered late, even if it is only one day past their due date. Never use the term 'grace period' when explaining when a late fee is assessed.
- The tenant should initial their next due date, and the portion of the lease agreement that explains the late fees.
 They should also initial that they understand the lien schedule and how it works.

Encourage them to put it on their calendar at home and on their phone. Let them know that some customers actually set an alert on their phone when their payment is due.
- o Do not allow the tenant to tell you they had no idea when their payment is due.
- o Explain that when people refrain from paying their rent, it is possible their goods may be sold at an auction
- Review the lease agreement again, before the customer leaves the office
    - o The lease is an important document that must be understood and followed by all. Understanding the agreement will hopefully prevent any future misunderstandings and will translate into a successful partnership

BONUS!

Using Auto-Debit to Reduce Collections

One of the most effective ways to reduce your collections effort is to sell tenants on the convenience of signing up for your auto-debit program.

Tenants who sign up for auto-debit:
- Tend to stay longer
- Tend to be more resistant to rent increases
- Are less of a collections problem

Learn to increase your auto-debit participation by using the yes-or-yes sales presentation. Instead of asking a tenant 'do you want to sign up for auto-debit?', instead say: 'Our customers love the convenience of our no-late-fee guarantee auto-debit program; would you prefer to use your Visa or MasterCard?'

In this case, you are not asking a 'yes-or-no' question ('Do you want to sign up for auto-debit?') but are instead of asking a 'yes-or-yes' question – whether they choose to use their Visa or Mastercard, they are an auto-debit customer!

Chapter 7

Effective Tools to Getting It All Done

'Time is what we want the most, but what we use the worst'...William Penn

A self-storage professional is able to utilize proven sales skills to rent more space and systematic collection techniques to collect more rent. All of this must be done using effective time management skills. Without those valuable skills, managers find themselves frustrated, inefficient and likely to burn out over a period of time.

Where do you find the time?

The first step in developing effective time management techniques is to compile a list of tasks one typically does each day. Once the list is compiled, calculate how long it takes to do each of those tasks:

- Break down an 8 hour day
    - Leases
        - Showing a unit
        - Explain the lease

- - - Enter into computer system
  - Vacates
    - Sweep out the unit
    - Remove rental from computer system
    - File away vacate paperwork
  - Trucks and merchandise
    - Prepare truck rental paperwork
    - Inspect truck
    - Re-stock sold merchandise
  - Paperwork
    - Daily reports
    - Deposit slips
- Go to the bank
- Eat lunch
- How long does it take to complete each of these tasks?
  - Based on previous experiences, how much time did it take to do the tasks? Get an average.

- In all likelihood, you will find two or three hours each day which you will not be able to account for

Learning with a Time Management Exercise

Some experts say if we do something for thirty days it will then become a habit. Whether dieting, budgeting, or trying to quit smoking, we have a greater chance of being successful if we stick to it. Using your time more efficiently is also a learned behavior.

- Divide your day into thirty-minute segments
  - On a blank sheet of paper, make a chart of the day, listing every thirty minutes from opening to closing.
- Document your activities throughout the day
  - Starting when you open your facility, document every thirty-minutes until you close.
- Keep a log for thirty days

- After thirty days, analyze your log. Look for gaps where you cannot account for time. Now look for portions of your day that were not as productive as you would like—time that wasn't spent renting space, collecting, or maintaining the property.
- Based on what you saw, what steps can you now take to make your next thirty days more productive?

Time Management Tips

In observing countless managers over the years, patterns have emerged in managers with excellent time management skills. The more we observed, the more we realized how much they had in common. They were highly productive, had a positive attitude about their work, and were much less likely to suffer burn out. Highly effective managers had a higher retention rate and fewer customer service issues. They found solutions instead of making excuses, and embraced challenges when they arose.

Those managers also had higher expectations for themselves than did their counterparts.

Common Characterizes

- Made good use of their downtime
- Most self-storage managers work well when business is booming. They can rent a large number of units, check in trucks, and sell boxes with ease. The struggle is with the downtime. When the business flow slows down, so does the effectiveness.
    - Clean vacant space immediately. A common time waster is allowing vacant spaces to go for long periods of time without being cleaned and made rent-ready. Efficient managers clean vacant spaces as soon as the units become vacant

- Prepare truck paperwork early in the week
    - A busy truck rental property manager can manage his/her time more effectively by preparing some of the truck rental paperwork in advance. Make sure the inspection sheets are filled out, and the reservations are read. Some managers are prone to wait until the last minute to get rental trucks ready and then things start to back up
- Keep leases readily available
    - Some managers still keep the various lease documents separated instead of keeping lease packets readily available. Keep all forms together and ready to use.
- Work smarter, not harder
    - Take locks on property tour

- - Smart professional self-storage managers take the locks with them on the property tour instead of waiting to bring up the lock requirement when they return to the office.
  - By taking the locks with them, they sell more locks and they are more effective with their time – they don't have to make a second trip out to the unit.
- Pick up trash on lock check
  - Inefficient managers make multiple trips onto the property instead of consolidating the tasks and trips. Effective managers pick up trash at the same time they conduct their lock check. They take a broom when they go out to check on a vacated space
- Schedule tasks
  - Effective managers have a schedule for their day-to-day tasks and stick to it as much as possible.

-
    - This includes collection calls, lock checks, and bank runs
- Write things down
    - A major source of wasted or lost time is the inability of many managers to keep track of items that need to be addressed
    - Many times, customer service issues that are not immediately addressed will become much larger issues that end up taking up far too much time.
    - Efficient managers return calls and deal with the caller's issue immediately.
- Do things right the first time!
    - The most efficient managers know that if they don't take the time to do something right they will be forced to make time to fix the problem. Excellent customer service means being proactive, not reactive. Take care of the small issues before they become larger ones.

- - An efficient manager keeps promises. Professionals live up to their word and live with the consequences of those promises.
- Share Responsibilities
    - The most efficient self-storage operations are managed by a team, with everyone doing their part each day. Failure to carry out those duties will harm the efficiency of a self-storage facility.
    - Clear communication
        - If a management team is working as efficiently as it should be, there will not be a duplication of work.

Conclusion

If you are the onsite manager of a self-storage facility you have a great deal of responsibility for the success of your facility. Unlike working in a large retail store or factory where there are large numbers of employees, it is highly likely that you are oftentimes the only person on duty at your site. Your ability to rent space, collect money and get it all done using effective time management are going to be the factors that determine whether or not your facility meets its expectations.

'Learning from the successful' is the first and most important step in your transition from a property care-taker to a self-storage professional. Your willingness to learn new skills, practice new techniques and utilize new ideas will increase both your value to the company you work for and the market competitiveness of the facility you manage.

Keep working to increase your ability to rent space even when it is a challenge.

Keep working to increase your effectiveness in collecting rent even when you would rather be doing something else. And keep working on perfecting your time management skills so you can get it all done, get it all done well and have a rich and rewarding life outside of storage.

Happy Renting and Collecting!

Bob Copper
Self Storage 101
866-269-1311
www.selfstorage101.com

Made in the USA
San Bernardino, CA
24 March 2016